CHILDREN'S AUTHORS

SHARON CREECH

Jill C. Wheeler

Checkerboard
Library

An Imprint of Abdo Publishing
www.abdopublishing.com

www.abdopublishing.com

Published by Abdo Publishing, a division of ABDO, PO Box 398166, Minneapolis, Minnesota 55439. Copyright © 2015 by Abdo Consulting Group, Inc. International copyrights reserved in all countries. No part of this book may be reproduced in any form without written permission from the publisher. Checkerboard Library™ is a trademark and logo of Abdo Publishing.

Printed in the United States of America, North Mankato, Minnesota.
102014
012015

Cover Photo: photo by Lyle Rigg
Interior Photos: Dan Chung/The Guardian p. 21; iStockphoto p. 7; photos courtesy of Sharon
     Creech pp. 5, 9, 11, 15, 16, 19
Absolutely Normal Chaos Cover Art (c) 2012 by Zdenko Basic. COVER Design (c) by
     HARPERCOLLINS PUBLISHERS. Used by permission of HarperCollins Publishers p. 13
Walk Two Moons COVER ART COPYRIGHT (c) 2012 by Zdenko Basic. COVER COPYRIGHT
     (c) by HARPERCOLLINS PUBLISHERS. Used by permission of HarperCollins Publishers
     p. 14
The Wanderer Cover Art (c) 2012 by Zdenko Basic. Used by permission of HarperCollins
     Publishers. p. 17

Series Coordinator: Bridget O'Brien
Editors: Heidi M.D. Elston, Megan M. Gunderson
Art Direction: Neil Klinepier

Library of Congress Cataloging-in-Publication Data

Wheeler, Jill C., 1964-
  Sharon Creech / Jill C. Wheeler.
     pages cm. -- (Children's Authors)
  Includes bibliographical references and index.
  ISBN 978-1-62403-666-8
1. Creech, Sharon--Juvenile literature. 2. Authors, American--20th century--Biography--Juvenile
literature. 3. Children's stories--Authorship--Juvenile literature. I. Title.
  PS3553.R3373Z94 2015
  813'.54--dc23
  [B]
                    2014025378

CONTENTS

Love That Author

Sharon Creech is best known for her novels aimed at middle-graders and young adults. She is the first American to win both the **Newbery Medal** from the **American Library Association** and Great Britain's **Carnegie Medal**. Creech won the 1995 Newbery for *Walk Two Moons* and the 2002 Carnegie for *Ruby Holler*.

Part of the reason Creech is so popular is that she seems to understand what it is like to be young. Her characters deal with problems similar to those her readers are going through. These include first loves, losing loved ones, going to school, and dealing with relatives.

Creech grew up with a passion for reading and writing. Yet she spent many years teaching literature before she began writing it. It was not until her children were in high school that she began putting her stories on paper. She loves stories, words, and creating something from nothing.

Creech has not let success change what is important to her. Spending time with her family is still her favorite thing. However, writing stories is her second favorite. She admits most of her stories come from who she is, what she's done, and what she's seen. Fortunately, her readers find those things pretty interesting!

Creech really gets into her characters. She has joked that if anyone talked to her while she was writing, she would probably sound like a seventh grader!

STORYTELLING FAMILY

Sharon Creech was born on July 29, 1945, in a **suburb** of Cleveland, Ohio. She had an older sister, Sandy. Her three younger brothers were Dennis, Doug, and Tom. Their parents were Arvel and Ann Creech. Arvel was an accountant. Ann was an office manager.

Sharon's household was noisy and rowdy. Friends and relatives often visited. Sharon's family did a lot of storytelling. She quickly learned to stretch her stories to make them more interesting.

Besides storytelling, the Creech family enjoyed traveling. They took a road trip nearly every year. They would go to Michigan or Wisconsin or visit cousins in Kentucky. Once they went to Idaho, spending five days on the road.

When her family wasn't traveling, Sharon liked playing outside, climbing trees, and riding her bike. She thought about becoming an ice skater, a singer, or a painter. However, she often fell on the ice. She could not sing very well. And, her drawing skills were limited.

Most of all, Sharon loved reading and writing. She especially loved Greek and Native American mythology. She also liked to collect writing instruments, including pens and paper. She loved the first day of school because she had new writing supplies.

Cleveland, Ohio

FINDING A CALLING

Sharon attended school in the Cleveland area. In 1963, she graduated from Charles H. Brush High School in South Euclid, Ohio. She then **enrolled** at Hiram College in Hiram, Ohio. It was the same college her sister, Sandy, had gone to.

During college, Sharon took many English, literature, and writing classes. The classes made her even more interested in storytelling. For a time, she considered becoming a reporter. However, she knew reporters had to stick to the facts. In her stories, if Sharon did not like the facts, she changed them!

Sharon graduated from Hiram in 1967 with a **degree** in English literature and writing. That same year, she married HR Leuthy Jr. They had a son, Rob, in 1968. Their daughter, Karin, was born in 1971.

In 1973, the family moved to Washington, DC. Sharon enrolled at George Mason University to work on a master's degree. While in graduate school, she worked at the Federal

Sharon and her children, Karin (left) and Rob (right)

Theater Project Archives in Fairfax, Virginia. The archives told the story of the Federal Theater Project, which provided work for people who needed jobs during the **Great Depression**.

Working around so many reminders of the theater got Sharon thinking about writing plays. Yet between work, school, and raising a family, she had little time to do that.

In Praise of Chaos

Two years after returning to England, Creech received sad news. Her father, Arvel, had passed away. He had suffered a **stroke** six years earlier. It had left him unable to talk.

Creech thought of all the words that had been trapped inside Arvel. It inspired her to write again. She started her first novel just a month after his death. The words just poured out.

Creech's first break as a writer came in 1987. She entered a poem in a contest. She won first place and $1,000! Winning the contest helped Creech realize people might enjoy reading what she wrote.

Creech decided to focus on writing novels. In 1990, she published an adult novel in England titled *The Recital*. The following year, she published another serious novel called *Nickel Malley*.

Creech wanted to write something funny, too. So, she wrote the journal of a 13-year-old girl who has an unusually crazy summer. *Absolutely Normal Chaos* was first published in England in 1990. Creech thought it would be for adults, but it became a successful young adult novel.

Creech had never planned to write for young people. She researched children's books after her publisher decided *Chaos* was best for younger readers. She quickly discovered her writing was ideal for that audience.

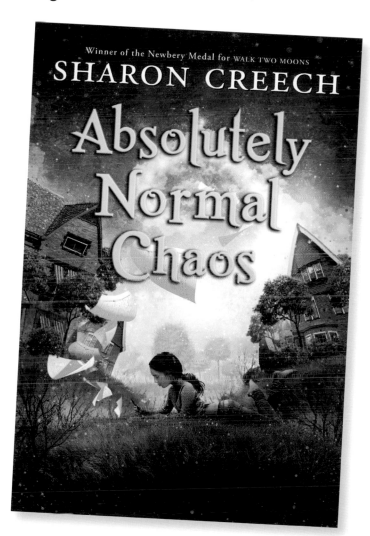

Creech modeled the family in Absolutely Normal Chaos after her own experiences. She even named the girl's brothers after her own brothers!

BACK TO AMERICA

American readers first learned about Creech in 1994 with her next book, *Walk Two Moons*. Building on her own childhood road trips, Creech wrote about another 13-year-old girl. She journeys to Idaho with her grandparents to visit the mother who left her.

In 1995, Creech received a call telling her *Walk Two Moons* had won a **Newbery Medal**! This award let Creech write full-time. It also made her a celebrity in America among fans of children's literature.

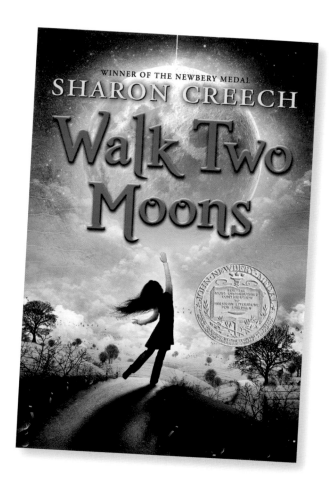

Walk Two Moons *was inspired by a fortune cookie! Creech's fortune said, "Don't judge a man until you've walked two moons in his moccasins."*

14

Creech won the Sequoyah Young Adults Book Award in 1997.
Kids vote and determine the winner of this award.

Then, Creech won a nomination for England's famous
Whitbread Award. It was for her 1997 novel *Chasing Redbird*.
The book is about a 13-year-old girl who discovers a trail
near her home that was once used by trappers and Native
Americans.

In 2001, Creech received a **Newbery Honor** award for her book *The Wanderer*. It is the story of a young girl and her cousin and their journey across the Atlantic Ocean on a sailboat.

Creech's office in Pennington, New Jersey

Creech's daughter, Karin, inspired the book. After graduating from college, Karin and six others sailed across the Atlantic. A bad storm hit and they nearly did not make it to Ireland. Creech decided to write a story about Karin's trip.

Creech and her family made their own journey across the Atlantic in 1998. They returned to the United States to settle in Pennington, New Jersey. That same year, Creech published the novel *Bloomability*.

Bloomability is about a girl who must adjust to a new life at a boarding school in Switzerland. Creech knew what life was like at a boarding school from her teaching experience. But, she still had to research the details. When it was published, *Bloomability* was another hit with readers.

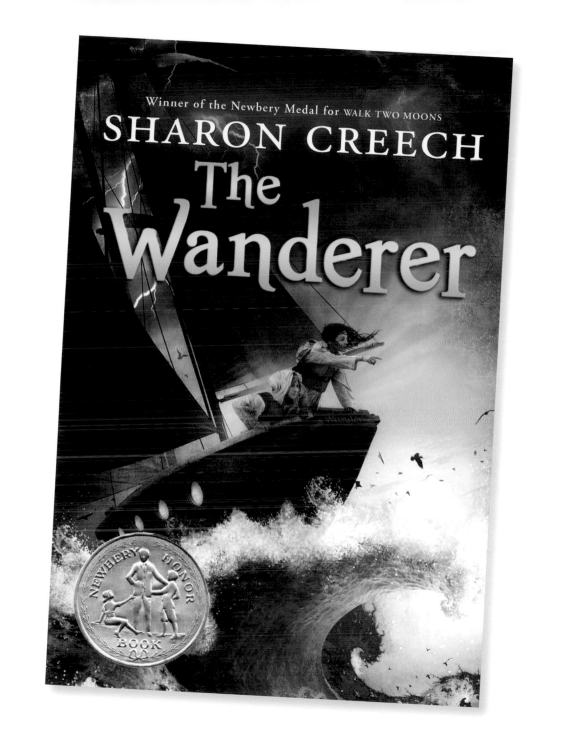

Poetry & Picture Books

Creech's successful writing career followed her to America. She had published novels for adults and children. She even had a play **produced**. But, her next projects took her in a slightly different direction.

Creech created a picture book for very young children in 2000. *Fishing in the Air* is the story of a boy who learns about his father's childhood while they are fishing. It was illustrated by Chris Raschka.

Creech used her teaching experiences in another picture book, *A Fine, Fine School*. The pictures were by Harry Bliss. It is the story of a principal who loves teaching so much he eventually asks his students to go to school on weekends, in summers, and even on holidays.

Before she began writing fiction, Creech had been a poet. So in 2001, she tried something new with *Love That Dog.* It is the story of a boy who uses poetry to help him deal with the death of a beloved dog. The novel is written in **free verse** as a series of poems in a student's journal.

Reaction to *Love That Dog* was positive. Readers loved it! Critics praised Creech's work to help young readers appreciate poetry. The book was so popular Creech wrote a **sequel** to it in 2008. It was cleverly titled *Hate That Cat*.

Love That Boy, *a poem by Walter Dean Myers (right), inspired Creech's novel* Love That Dog.

Fiction, Not Facts

With all her writing success, Creech no longer teaches. But, she credits some of that success to teaching literature. It helped her understand what makes a great story. She also feels being a parent and grandparent has helped her writing.

Her recent novels include *The Great Unexpected*, *Ruby Holler*, *Replay*, *The Castle Corona*, and *The Boy on the Porch*. The picture book *Granny Torrelli Makes Soup* and the novel *Heartbeat* were both inspired by her first grandchild.

Today, Creech and her husband live in Camden, Maine. She is in her office writing and responding to fans from eight thirty in the morning until about noon. She loves working in her pajamas! After lunch, she takes a walk and then works again until dinner.

New stories tend to sneak up on Creech just as she is finishing the current one! Once she starts a new book, Creech may spend ten hours a day letting the characters speak and the

Creech says reading great stories makes her want to write great stories. Her favorite authors include Virginia Woolf, Walter Dean Myers, and Christopher Paul Curtis.

story develop. Then, she finishes the whole first draft before she begins **revisions**. She may revise a **manuscript** four or five times before sending it to her editor.

On average, Creech's books take about a year to write. Best of all, she can change the facts as much as she wants!

GLOSSARY

American Library Association - an organization whose goal is to promote library and information services.

Carnegie Medal - a British award that is given each year to the author of an outstanding children's book.

degree - a title given by a college to its students for completing their studies.

enroll - to register, especially in order to attend a school.

free verse - an open form of poetry that does not use consistent patterns or rhymes.

Great Depression - the period from 1929 to 1942 of worldwide economic trouble. There was little buying or selling, and many people could not find work.

headmaster - the man in charge of a school, such as a principal.

manuscript - a handwritten or typed book or article not yet published.

Newbery Medal - an annual award given by the American Library Association. It honors the author of the best American children's book published in the previous year. A Newbery Honor Book is a runner-up to the Newbery Medal.

produce - to oversee the making of a movie, a play, an album, or a radio or television show.

revise - to change something in order to correct or improve it.

sequel (SEE-kwuhl) - a book, movie, or other work that continues the story begun in a preceding one.

stroke - a sudden loss of sensation, voluntary motion, and mental activity. It is caused by the breaking of a blood vessel in the brain.

suburb - a town, village, or community just outside a city.

Whitbread Award - an award sponsored by the Whitbread Breweries. It is now called the Costa Book Award. It is given to books that are well written and popular among a wide range of readers.

WEBSITES

To learn more about Children's Authors, visit **booklinks.abdopublishing.com**. These links are routinely monitored and updated to provide the most current information available.

INDEX